Sculptural Boxes

made easy

volume 1

A hands on approach to creating
uniquely beautiful boxes with basic
woodworking tools

Thomas H. Haapapuro Jr.

Dedication

This book is dedicated to my fantastic wife, Erin, for the support and patience she gives me each and every day. This book is also dedicated to my family, for the assistance they have all made to my development along the way. Thank you.

I would also like to thank my professors at The Ohio State University, especially J. Brooks Breeden, who told me to publish, publish, publish. My unwavering thanks.

Working with wood, and the tools used to work it, is inherently dangerous, especially if the tools are used incorrectly. Some images were shot in a manner best suited for clarity of the process, and may not represent the safest way to operate the tools. Neither the author nor the publisher assumes any liability for the safety of the reader. This book is sold without warranties or guarantees of any kind, expressed or implied, and the author disclaims any liability for any injuries, losses, or damages caused in any way by the content of this book or the reader's use of the tools needed to complete the projects presented herein. The author urges all readers to thoroughly review each project and to understand the use of all tools before beginning any project. Safety is the most important skill of any woodworker.

about the author

Thomas Haapapuro is a landscape architect and an artist. His art work spans a variety of materials, forms, and uses. He is particularly fond of using native wood from salvaged trees. These materials connect people with the landscape and the flora of the local environment, as well as reduce the carbon footprint in the process of making art.

Originally from the rural Appalachian foothills of eastern Ohio, this natural environment fused in him a deep appreciation of natural shapes and forms, which inform his work.

This is the second book by Thomas. His first book, *Fresh Designs for Woodworking* by Fox Chapel Publishing, introduced readers to his scroll saw based wood art. He has also written several articles for Scroll Saw Magazine.

Thomas also creates a line of organically shaped carved wood bowls which are in private collections throughout the united states. To see these bowls, visit www.modernwoodbowls.com

Thomas lives with his wife Erin in Charlotte, North Carolina.

Introduction

A box is an simple object, generally defined as a vessel with a lid, meant to contain or obscure smaller objects. That is it. Everything else is left open to the imagination. It can be any material, any size, any shape. It is the simplest object a wood worker can create. As a simple object with a reductive definition, it is the most ubiquitous project for wood workers the world over. Whole books have been written showcasing just how many wide and varied interpretations on the box exist in the world. So simple a project, and as its goals are so simple, the possibilities to explore this object are wide open to the flights of imagination.

Woodwork is traditionally viewed as a rectangular art form. The boards are flat. The corners are 90 degrees. The form is boxy (pun intended). Certainly, a lot of the tools of the trade, if used in the traditional ways, lend to rectilinearity. But this need not be. A few tricks and a little vision can transform a basic wood working project into a unique and stylish work of art. That is what this book will teach you, how to transform a stack of square lumber into an exciting, fluid and organic work of art.

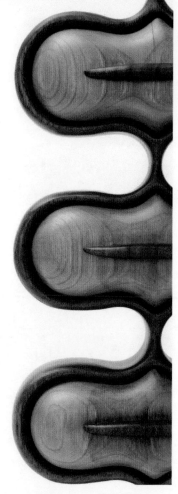

TABLE OF CONTENTS

Project Guide

Vertical Ascension
13

Rising Sun
24

Retro Ascension
28

Opposing Forces
34

Sprout
36

The Giving Tree
38

Modern Ascension
30

Oscillating Ascension
32

Tribalism
41

Congruent Waves
45

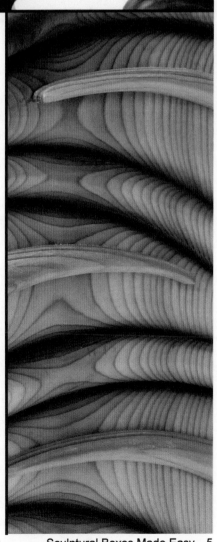

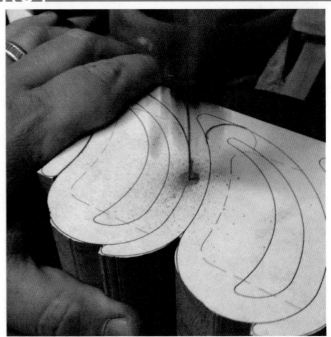

BEFORE WE BEGIN

Before getting started, it is helpful to go over the basics of the tools and materials we will be using throughout the book.

Tools

We will be using several different types of tools to create the boxes in this book, but most of them are tools that are typically present in most wood shops. The primary tools we will be using is the band saw and the scroll saw. These two tools combined can create amazing, beautiful works of wooden art. In this chapter, we will overview the tools I used to create each of the boxes in this book.

Band Saw

The band saw is a staple of the wood shop. It can be used to rip cut lumber to a thinner dimension and cut out curvilinear shapes. It is also the most powerful tool in the wood shop arsenal. A lot of the projects in this book could be cut entirely with a scroll saw, but it is not as fast a cutting tool as the band saw, so whenever possible we will use the band saw to cut the majority of the box. We will also use the band saw to rip cut wood to the proper dimension, and to slice the fronts and backs off the drawer blanks.

The blades used for the projects varies between tasks. Rip cutting is best done with a wider blade,

typically 1/2" to 3/4". The wider blade aids in getting a straighter rip cut, leaving less warp in the cut and a cleaner project. For cuts where greater agility is required, such as cutting the outside shape of the box body, a smaller width blade is best. I typically use a 1/4" blade, though anywhere from a 1/8" blade to a 3/8" blade will work. For both the wide blades and the thin blades, select a blade that has the highest TPI (tooth per inch) available. More teeth means a somewhat slower cutting rate, but it gives a much cleaner, smoother cut.

Scroll Saw

Most wood shops also have the band saws little cousin, the scroll saw. Often seen as a tool for cutting smaller projects like creating fretwork, intarsia and other detailed projects, the scroll saw has a some definite advantages:

- **Finger safe**: The worst injury likely with this little saw is a minor finger cut. So for very close cutting, like drawer pulls, I prefer to have by fingers next to a scroll saw blade than a band saw, though a band saw can be safely used if care is taken. It is just a preference of risk avoidance on my part.

- **Thin kerf:** The blades on a scroll saw are much thinner than a band saw blade. Hence, the kerf (the gap left by the saw blade in the cut wood) is much narrower. This allows for much tighter drawers. Tighter drawers, meaning the gap between the drawer and the box body, not only look cleaner and more professional, but they also sag much less when the drawer is opened.

- **Tight corners:** Even with an 1/8" blade on the band saw, it can only turn 1/8" radius, which is fine for some projects, but it is still a limitation. With the scroll saw and the right blades, there is virtually no restriction on the size turns that can be made.

- **Inside cuts**: This is the primary advantage of the scroll saw over any other tool. With a scroll saw, a hole can be drilled into the wood and then the blade can be threaded through it. This ability makes a wide range of projects possible. If the band saw was used exclusively, the projects would need to be designed to have an access path from the outside of the box to the inside where the drawers are cut. Some of the projects in this book could be done this way, but some of the projects would simply not be possible without the unique capabilities of the scroll saw.

Power Carvers

To transform a standard box to a sculptural box, the box will require carving. Carving in this case though is a relatively basic technique. Our goal will be to simply round over the edges of the box, drawers, and other components. This work can be done with a wide arrange of tools depending on what tools are available and the wood worker's preference.

Rotary Tools

One option are rotary bits. These include burr bits that fit into rotary tools (Dremel, Foredom). These can be used very successfully in the boxes in this book. In my experience, a drum bit with a lower

TPI is best for long, straight edges, such as the edges of the drawer or the outside of the box. Ball burr bits, again with a low TPI, can be very useful in inside corners. Great care must be taken using burr bits though, as they can jump and bite if care is not taken, especially when carving against end grain.

King Arthur's Tools - The Merlin

King Arthur's Tools (**www.katools.com**) makes one of my personal favorite tools and the tool used in every one of the boxes in this book, the Merlin. The Merlin is a small angle grinder that comes with a wide array of attachments perfect for sculptural box making. These attachments include a small chain saw blade, which can be used to quickly knock the corners off the boxes and drawers. It also comes with a bur disk, which is perfect for refining the edges and getting the pieces ready for sanding. It also comes with sanding disks if you prefer to power sand your boxes.

Due disclosure. After using the KA Tools products for years in my wood work and articles, they invited me to represent them at a local wood working tool expo. Since I already loved their product line, I agreed. Many years on, I continue to represent their tools at wood working shows. I now know the people who operate this family business, and we have a great relationship. But no matter how wonderful the people and the company is, it all started because I fell in love with the amazing high quality tools they make. You will see their tools pictured in many of the process images in this book, not because of my relationship with the company, but because the tools really are the best suited to the projects.

Planers

Re-sawn wood, rip cut wood, and oversized wood will all need to be milled flat with a planer. To be honest, for this book, I planed the back board of the boxes down to 1/4", then taped it into place. You could cut the back of the box off with the band saw, but I prefer to have a perfectly flat board on the back, rather than a somewhat rougher cut board at the back. But either approach is acceptable.

Sanding

Ughh. Sanding. To many wood workers, sanding can be the most tedious part of the wood working experience. However, I have met a few who actually enjoy the Zen like process of sanding. To those of you who find sanding a satisfying and calming activity, good for you. Let me know if you want to sand some of my work.

For the rest of you, sanding can be made a lot less time consuming by using a power sanding system. There are many of these on the market, but again, King Arthur Tools gets my vote. Their Guinevere sander is a sanding system built around a motor and a flexible shaft. In the shaft, pneumatic sanding drums with a sanding sleeve are used. The drums come in many different sizes and shapes, allowing the wood worker to power sand nearly any corner, nook or cranny. Power sanding saves a lot of time and energy, and allows the wood worker to move quickly past this daunting step in the wood art process.

In this book we will also use belt sanders for rough shaping. My preference is a stand up 1" belt sander. This tool is much less aggressive than a 4" belt sander, and allows more intricate shaping tasks, such as rough shaping the drawer pulls.

Accessories

In addition to the tools and the wood, there are several other items that will be helpful in creating the boxes. A brief list is provided below:

Glue

All the boxes will need to be glued. Every wood worker has their preference, and mine is Titebond II. It has a fast initial tack and a relatively quick curing time, and it is strong.

Double Sided Tape

A quality paper based double sided tape is absolutely critical to creating these boxes. In this book, it is typically used to temporarily hold pieces together as they are cut, when they can then be separated again after the cut. This technique is used in every project in this book. Double sided tape can be purchased at any wood working store, though I have always purchased mine from Klingspor Wood Working Shop (www. woodworkingshop.com)

Sharpened Putty Knife

Related to the double sided tape is the sharpened putty knife, as I use this to separate the pieces of wood held together with the double sided tape. I find that a metal putty knife, sharpened to a knife edge on a whetstone, is perfect to separate pieces of wood that are taped together. The thin edge nicely gets between the layers of wood, and the narrow blade allows the pieces to be pried apart without damaging or denting the wood.

Clamps

A wood worker can never have enough clamps. For this book, clamps will be used routinely as pieces are glued together. Largely two types will be used, bar clamps and spring clamps. Bar clamps are best to assemble the larger bodies of the box. Spring clamps are a great way to secure the drawers during glue up.

Wood Selection

Any kind of wood can be used to create the boxes in this e book. To show the variety of woods that can be used, I have elected to make the boxes from a wide array of different woods.

Soft Woods

Generally, soft woods are easier to sculpt. These include pine, cedar, and some maples, to name but a few. These woods are the best choice for beginners, as they are often more affordable and are significantly easier to cut.

One readily available source for soft woods is cedar fence planks sold at any of the big box hardware stores. It is typically rough sawn, so it will first need to be planed, but it is a very affordable material, is very easy to work, and makes a very attractive box. This wood was used to make the Vertical Ascension box and the Opposing Forces box.

Hard Woods

Hard woods, such as oak, walnut, and cherry are intuitively harder to carve. If you are using the chain saw carvers, this isn't much of a hurdle. If you are using rotary bits though, hard woods can be a daunting material to carve. Hard woods are my personal favorite, especially Walnut and Cherry. While they are harder to carve, they are dramatic and beautiful woods, especially when paired together. Most of the boxes in this book were made from Walnut and Cherry.

Manufactured Woods

Manufactured wood such as plywood also work well for these boxes. This wood gives a very interesting pattern when carved. The many layers of wood laminated together to make plywood really exaggerate shape and form when carved. If you decide to try plywood for these boxes, I recommend cabinet grade pine based plywood. Cabinet grade plywood generally has less voids and gaps in the laminated wood pieces, and will yield a better-looking box.

Wood Preparation

All of the boxes in this book are relatively thick, 3" or more in thickness. Most milled lumber is ¾" in thickness (excluding the cedar fence planks, which are generally 1/2" thick). So multiple pieces of lumber need to be assembled to create a block thick enough to make a box from. So start by cutting boards slightly wider and longer than the pattern of the box you intend to make. Glue the boards together, face-to-face. The block can be any thickness you decide of course, though I would keep the boxes between 3" or less. Since most of the boxes will be cut using the scroll saw, make sure that the block is not thicker than the scroll saw can cut. Apply glue to the faces of the wood boards, stack together, and clamp into place. Set aside to dry.

Match-booking a board is a technique that can give beautiful patterns to the edges of the boxes. Match-booking means that you cut two or three pieces of wood from a single board. The first board is cut, then the second board is cut, flipped over, so that the top of the first board and the bottom of the second board are both at the top. The same is done with the third and fourth board, etc. Below is an example:

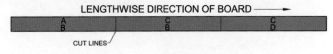

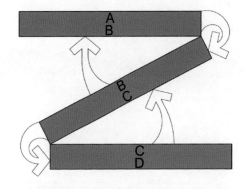

This technique was used on many of the boxes in this book, must notably on the Rising Sun box and on the Giving Tree box.

THE PROJECTS

All of the boxes in this book follow the same basic
process. To begin, this book will walk the reader
step by step for one particular box, providing
detailed images and instructions for each part
of the build. The rest of the book will be more
concise, leaving out the steps that are standard,
but will show the steps that are different and
unique to each box to guide the reader along.

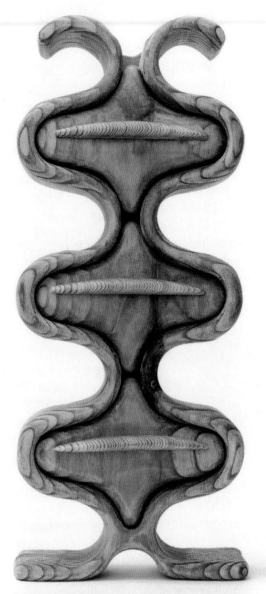

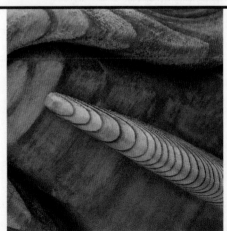

VERTICAL ASCENSION BOX

Building the Box

For this box, I used cedar wood (cedar fence planks actually), as it is a very easy wood to carve. But any wood could be used for any of the boxes in this book. Wood selection for the boxes is a factor of preference and what is available.

1 PLANE THE BOARDS

To begin, the boards are planed so that both sides of the board are flat. It is better to plane the board when it is long, rather than cutting it to the size of the intended box and then planing it. A longer board will have less snipe and will be more level.

2. CUT THE BOARDS TO SIZE

Once the board is planed, use a chop saw to cut the board into lengths a little bigger than the outside limits of the box. Ideally, the wood should be 1/4" bigger than the pattern on all sides. The boards are all cut in the image below. Since the boards used are relatively thin (1/2"), five of them are used to get the desired thickness.

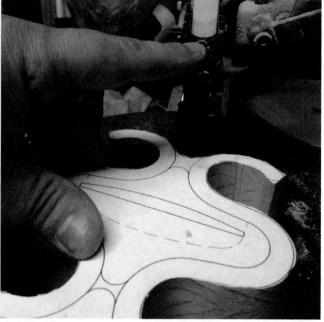

3. CHECK SCROLL SAW LIMITS

This is a good time to check the tool capabilities. The inner drawers on this box, like all the boxes in this book, will be cut with a scroll saw. So the maximum cutting depth of the scroll saw needs to be verified. Add or remove boards as necessary to ensure that the scroll saw will be able to cut the drawers once the bottom most board is removed.

Push the scroll saw arm down as far as it will go. This is the maximum cutting depth that the scroll saw can cut. For this saw, the maximum depth is 3". Note that to increase the cutting depth of a scroll saw, remove the hold down arm from the saw.

4. SQUARE THE BAND SAW

This is also a good time to check the band saw is perfectly square. Use a metal square to verify that the blade is precisely perpendicular to the table, and adjust if necessary.

5. RIP CUT THE BOTTOM BOARD

Using the band saw, cut the bottom board of the stack in half. Since the wood for this box is 1/2" thick material, this means setting the fence at 1/4"

6. REASSEMBLE THE RIP CUT BOARD

Place the board that was just cut with the cut side up. Attach a high quality double sided tape to the cut face of the board. Then place the other side of the cut board on top of the tape.

7. GLUE UP THE REST OF THE BLOCK

Spread glue on top of the last board which was taped together. Spread the glue in a ringed pattern to ensure that there is sufficient glue on all parts of the board. Then place another board on top of this board. Repeat this process until all the wood is stacked. Note. Do not put glue on the topmost board.

8. CLAMP AND DRY

Clamp all the boards together and set aside to dry. To summarize, the bottom two board are held together with double sided tape. The rest of the boards are bound with glue.

9. ATTACH PATTERN TO WOOD BLOCK

When the glue has dried (usually several hours), cut out the pattern. Use a temporary spray adhesive to attach the pattern to the top of the wood block. Spray the adhesive onto the back of the paper, not the wood block itself. This will make it easier later to remove the pattern.

10. CUT THE OUTSIDE EDGE OF THE BOX

Using a narrow blade in the band saw (1/4" blade is shown in the example, cut the outer limits of the box pattern, shown with a darker line in the pattern. Take your time and cut this line carefully.

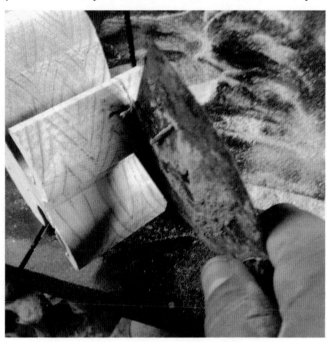

11. REMOVE THE BOTTOM TAPED BOARD

When the outer shape of the box is cut, use a putty knife to pry apart the bottom two boards, which are the two boards held together with the double sided tape.

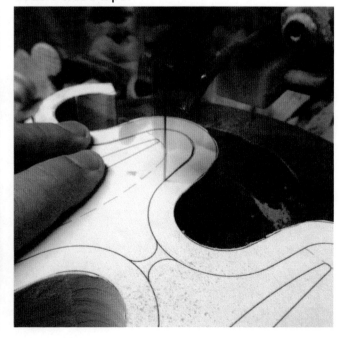

12. CUT THE DRAWER BLOCK

With the bottom board removed, the drawers can be cut from the box. Using a skip tooth blade in the scroll saw, cut the drawer blank from the box. As with the band saw, it is essential to check that the table is perpendicular to the blade on the scroll saw. Actually, it is even more important. If the table is not square, the drawer sides will be beveled, and will not be able to slide easily in and out of the box body. Take your time with this step, and do nut rush the cut. Rushing the cut will cause the saw blade to bow out inside the cut, which will leave a bulge in the drawer which will also make it difficult to pull the drawers in and out of the box body. Take your time.

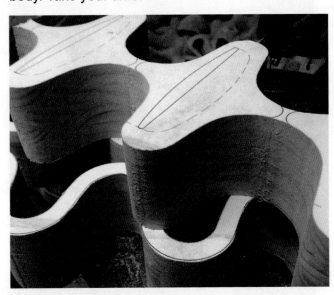

13. TESTING THE DRAWERS

Once the drawer blank has been cut, it should be able to pull smoothly from the box body.

14. ASSEMBLE THE BOX BODY

It is now time to reassemble the box body. Apply a ribbon of glue the back of the box body. Use a finger to spread the glue out evenly.

15. CLAMP AND LET DRY.

Turn the box over so the glue faces downward, and press it onto the back of the box which was removed earlier with the putty knife. Make sure to align the box carefully so that it lines up as closely as possible. Clamp the box together firmly and set aside to dry. (Notice the wood was book-matched)

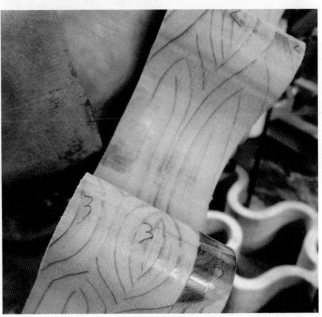

16. NUMBER THE DRAWER SIDES

While the box body is drying, we can work on the drawers. It can be very difficult to keep track of the drawers when they are cut free. For this reason, adding numbers to the sides of the drawers is very helpful. The numbers are added in triplicate so that we can keep track of the drawer pieces, front back and middle, when we cut the cavities from the drawers.

17. CUTTING THE DRAWERS

Use the scroll saw to cut the drawers free of the block. The little waste piece can be thrown away.

18. RIP CUT THE DRAWERS

Now it is time to cut the front and the back off of each drawer. Set the fence on the band saw about 1/4" from the blade, and carefully cut the front and back of the drawer. Do this for each of the drawers.

19. DRAW THE CAVITIES

This image shows the three pieces of the drawer that were made with the band saw in the previous step. Now, using a marker, trace the cut out pattern on the middle piece of the drawer. Use the band saw, and cut along this line. This will create the cavity in the drawer.

20. CUT THE DRAWER CAVITIES

The drawer should look like this after cutting. The smaller inside piece is waste and can be thrown away.

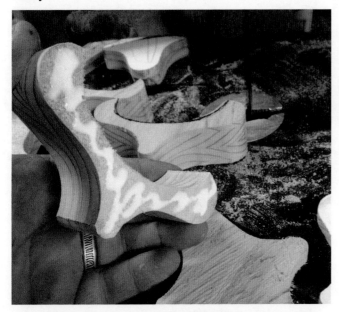

21. ASSEMBLING THE DRAWERS

With the cavity cut, it is time to reassemble the drawer. Apply glue to the back of the middle section of the drawer, and press onto the back of the drawer. Repeat this step to attach the front to the drawer. The numbers we drew earlier will ensure we have all the drawers properly matched. Clamp the drawer together, and set aside to dry. Spring clamps work well for this kind of clamping.

22 CUT THE DRAWER HANDLES

At this point everything is drying, so it is a good time to cut the drawer handles. Select a thinner piece of wood which matches the rest of the box. Attach the drawer handle pattern to the wood using spray adhesive. Make sure to align the pattern so that the wood grain in the handles will be going the same way the wood grain in the box was running, so that it looks consistent. Use the scroll saw to cut the handles from the wood.

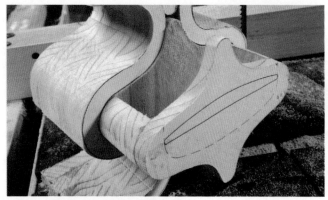

Carving the Box

Now that the box is built, we can begin carving the box. This is the step which transforms the project from a cool box to an amazing work of art. It may seem complicated, but by following the steps below, anyone can make a unique sculptural box.

For this box, we will be using the power carvers and sanders sold by King Arthur's Tools. As mentioned earlier in this book, a wide range of tools could be used, even basic rasps and sandpaper. I use King Arthur's tools because I have them, and because they offer a lot of control and significantly speed up the carving and sanding process.

23 DRAWING A CARVING AID

The first step is to draw a line on the front of the box, right down the middle. We will carve to this line. We could just knock the corners off the wood, but to make the box truly sculptural, we want to create a fully rendered 3d face to the box. So drawing a line down the middle and carving to that line will help make sure we are aggressive enough with the carving tools.

24 ROUGH CARVING THE BOX BODY

Using the carving tool of your choice, cut the edges off the box at about a 45 degree angle to the center line drawn in the step above. Do this all sides of the box, both inside and out, and on the back side as well. In the example above, the Merlin is used, first with the chain saw blade to remove the bulk of the material, then with the bur disk to refine the shape.

25 ROUGH CARVE THE DRAWERS

Carving the drawers takes a little more care. If the drawers are over-carved, the shape of the drawer will change. For that reason, it is important to leave about 1/8" to 1/4" of the inside edge of the drawer front unchanged. The graphic below demonstrates the approach:

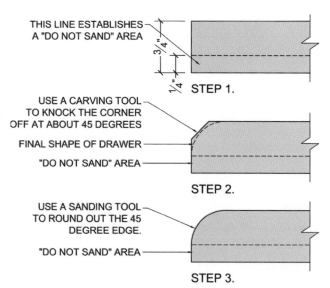

This image shows the rough carved drawer. The edges have been removed at about a 45 degree angle, but the inside edge of the drawer front was left untouched.

27 FINE SANDING

When rough sanding is complete, switch to a finer grained sandpaper and re-sand the box. Repeat this step again, gradually working up to at least 400 grit sandpaper for a smooth finish.

Even with power sanders, a little hand sanding may be necessary to get into tight corners and to smooth out some areas.

26 ROUGH SANDING

Power carves are great tools to get the rough shape established, but power sanders take it the rest of the way. Again, for this step, other tools could be used, such as rasps and sand paper. However, the Guinevere Sanding System by KA Tools is my preferred tool. In the image above, a sanding drum with 80 grit sand paper is being used on the box body to refine the shape.

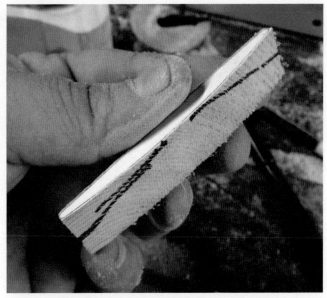

28 SHAPING THE HANDLES

Next we begin sculpting the drawer handles we cut earlier on the scroll saw. Using a marker, draw a line similar to the one shown in the image. Use a belt sander to remove the extra material. Use a power sander to round over the edges just as was done for the box body and drawers.

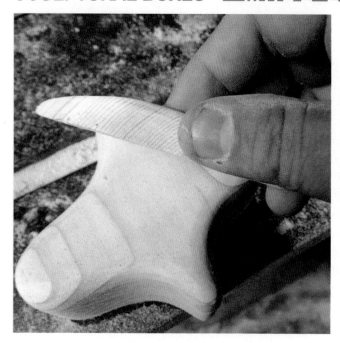

29 ATTACH THE HANDLES
Apply a think coat of glue to the back of the handle, and press it down onto the face of the drawer.

30 CLAMP THE HANDLES
Use spring clamps to hold the handles in place while the glue dries.

Finishing

Finishing materials and methods are a matter of preference. Many people like polyurethane sprays. These give a very durable finish and create a high shine. The drawback is that they do not penetrate the wood so do not bring out the full richness in color that an oil based finish will provide. Another option is a mixed finish of linseed oil and varnish. The oil saturates the wood and brings out its natural colors, and the varnish gives a stiff protective coating. A third option, and the one used for the projects in this book is a mix of beeswax and linseed oil. This can be wiped on with a cloth, then buffed out. The Guinevere system also features buffing sleeves that fit over the inflatable drums used to sand the pieces. I find this approach is more forgiving of small imperfections, and gives a wonderful satin finish.

SUMMARY

The rest of the projects in this book are essentially variations on this box, using the same basic techniques and processes. A few variations do occur with some of the boxes. For those boxes, a few images of the key steps will be provided to guide you through their construction.

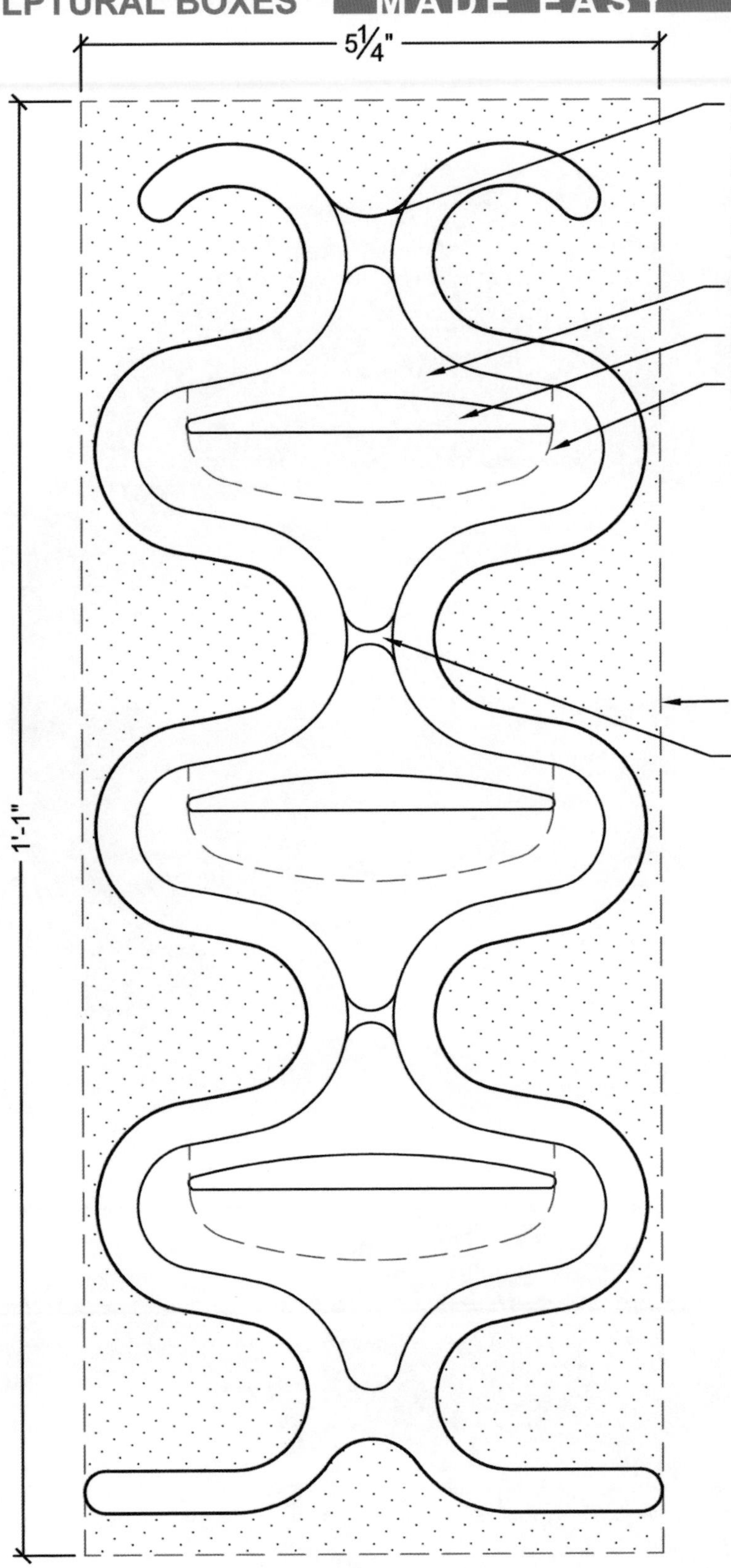

5¼"

DO NOT CUT THIS PART
WHEN CUTTING THE BOX
PERIMETER. IT IS CUT
WHEN THE DRAWERS ARE
CUT

DRAWER (TYP.)

DRAWER PULL (TYP.)

DRAWER CAVITY (TYP.)

EDGE OF WOOD BLOCK

WASTE MATERIAL (TYP.)

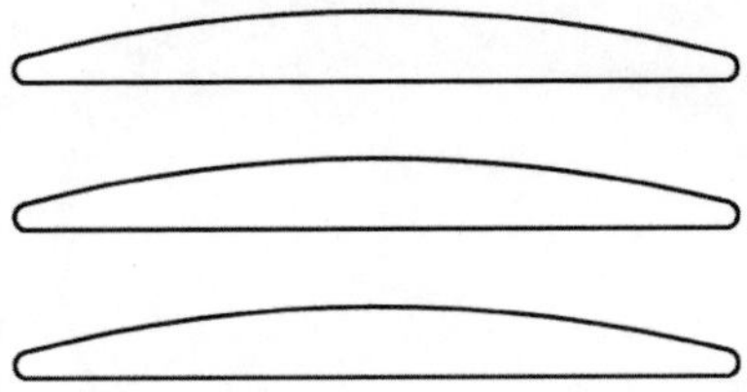

1'-1"

VERTICAL ASCENSION
PATTERN A
SCALE IMAGE UP BY 170%

DRAWER PULLS
PATTERN B

RISING SUN BOX

Key Steps

This single drawer box is a simple, elegant box that builds on the techniques used in the last box, but adds a couple additional tricks to the process. Unlike the last box, the drawer must be cut with the scroll saw, since it is an inside cut. This box is also shown with a walnut body and a cherry drawer front. This adds a lot of drama to the box, and is easy to create.

As before, prepare the lumber. Cut the outer edges of the box on the band saw. Remove the back panel from the box body, and we are ready to begin with the new process.

DRILL THE ACCESS HOLE
Note on the pattern an access hole has been shown. This will be the hole used to thread the scroll saw blade. It is best for this hole to be on the side or bottom of the drawer. Use a drill press to drill the hole so that the hole is perpendicular to the main box body.

CUT OUT THE DRAWER.
Thread the scroll saw blade through the access hole, secure it, then cut out the drawer. Be sure to be careful and go slowly as you cut. Do not push the blade, but let it have the time to cut the wood. Forcing the cut could cause the blade to warp, which could cause the cut to bow out. If this happens, it will be very difficult to remove the drawer from the box. A perpendicular, even cut is essential to success at this stage. I also find it helpful to let the blade idle in place for a few seconds before changing direction, such as going around the ends of the drawer. This gives the blade a chance to catch up, just in case the blade did get a little warped in the previous cut.

CUTTING THE FRONT AND BACK OF THE DRAWER.
As in the first box, use the band saw to cut about 1/4" off the front and back of the drawer blank. Then, trace a pocket onto the middle section with a marker. Use the band saw to cut the pocket, and throw away the waste material.

MAKING THE DRAWER FRONT.

In the first example, we kept the three pieces of the drawer, and glued them back together. For this box, we will change that slightly. Take the piece of wood that would normally be the front of the drawer, and lay it on a piece of cherry wood. Make sure to line the grain of the cherry wood with the grain of the walnut drawer front so that the grains match direction. Then, trace the shape of the drawer front onto the cherry wood. Then use the scroll saw to cut the drawer front shape traced on the cherry wood. Then, glue the drawer together. This makes the back of the drawer and the inside of the drawer walnut, and the face of the drawer cherry.

The thickness of the cherry board is up to your discretion. Generally, it is advisable for the cherry wood to be at least a little thicker than the walnut board it is replacing, to make up for the kerf removed when slicing the drawer into three pieces. An interesting effect can be obtained by using a piece of cherry wood much thicker than the board it replaced. The Retro Ascension box later in this book did just that. I used cherry wood that was nearly 3/4" thick to replace the 1/4" walnut board that was originally part of the drawer. Using a thicker contrasting wood gives a rounder, cloud-like appearance to the drawer front.

FINISHING THE BOX

From this point, follow the steps for the first box, including cutting the handle from a piece of walnut, and carving the box body, drawer, and handle.

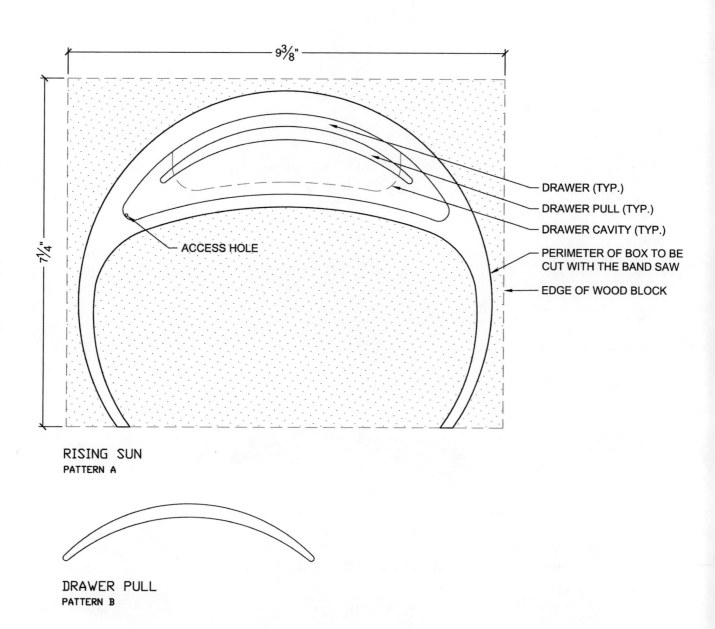

9³⁄₈"

7¹⁄₄"

DRAWER (TYP.)

DRAWER PULL (TYP.)

DRAWER CAVITY (TYP.)

PERIMETER OF BOX TO BE
CUT WITH THE BAND SAW

EDGE OF WOOD BLOCK

ACCESS HOLE

RISING SUN
PATTERN A

DRAWER PULL
PATTERN B

SCALE IMAGE UP BY 200%

MODERN ASCENSION BOX

PROJECT #3

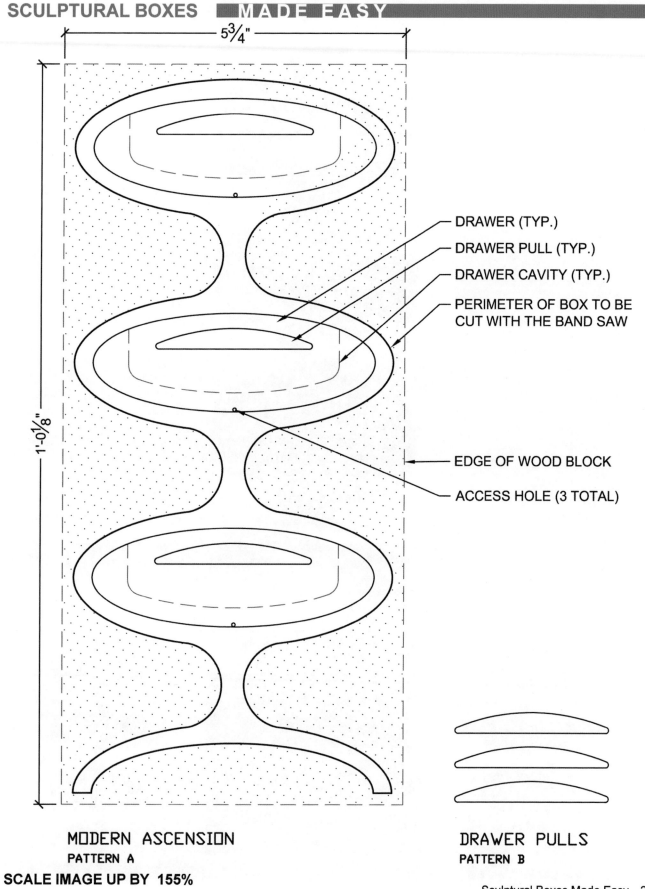

5³⁄₄"

1'-0¹⁄₈"

DRAWER (TYP.)

DRAWER PULL (TYP.)

DRAWER CAVITY (TYP.)

PERIMETER OF BOX TO BE
CUT WITH THE BAND SAW

EDGE OF WOOD BLOCK

ACCESS HOLE (3 TOTAL)

MODERN ASCENSION
PATTERN A
SCALE IMAGE UP BY 155%

DRAWER PULLS
PATTERN B

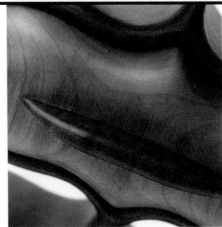

RETRO ASCENSION BOX

PROJECT #4

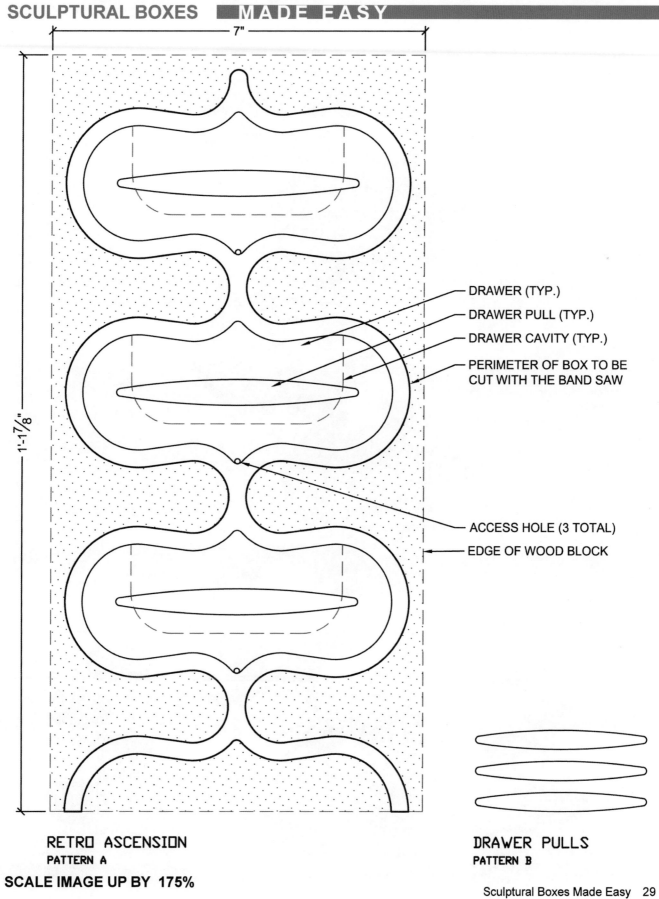

7"

1'-1⅞"

DRAWER (TYP.)

DRAWER PULL (TYP.)

DRAWER CAVITY (TYP.)

PERIMETER OF BOX TO BE
CUT WITH THE BAND SAW

ACCESS HOLE (3 TOTAL)

EDGE OF WOOD BLOCK

RETRO ASCENSION
PATTERN A

DRAWER PULLS
PATTERN B

SCALE IMAGE UP BY 175%

OSCILLATING ASCENSION BOX

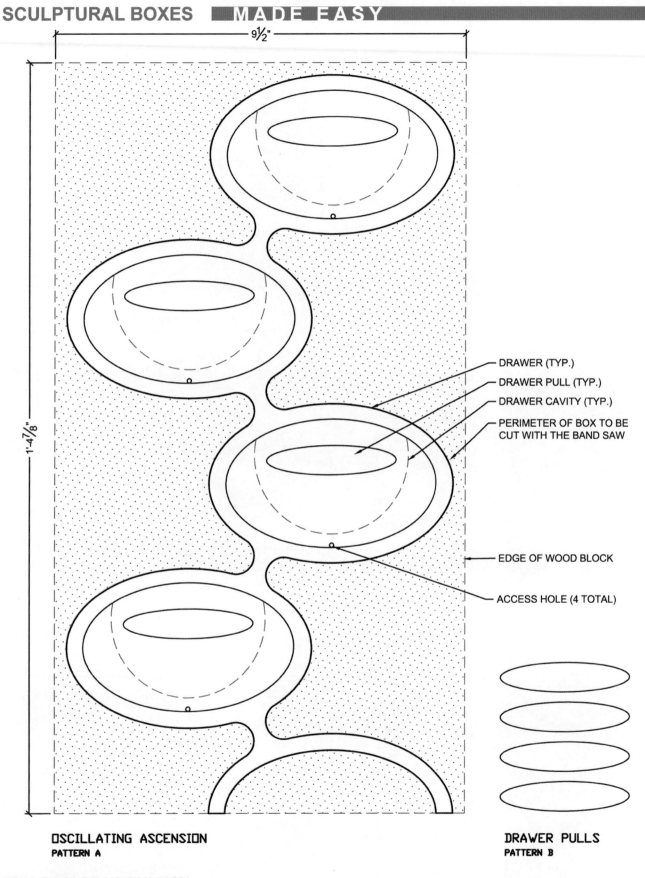

DRAWER (TYP.)

DRAWER PULL (TYP.)

DRAWER CAVITY (TYP.)

PERIMETER OF BOX TO BE
CUT WITH THE BAND SAW

EDGE OF WOOD BLOCK

ACCESS HOLE (4 TOTAL)

9½"

1'-4⅞"

OSCILLATING ASCENSION
PATTERN A

DRAWER PULLS
PATTERN B

SCALE IMAGE UP BY 210%

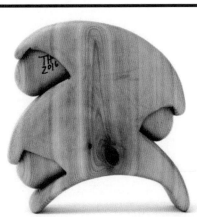

OPPOSING FORCES BOX

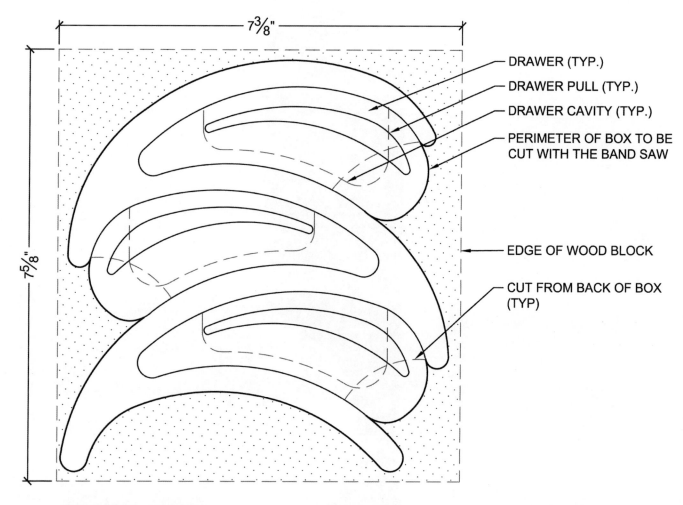

DRAWER (TYP.)

DRAWER PULL (TYP.)

DRAWER CAVITY (TYP.)

PERIMETER OF BOX TO BE
CUT WITH THE BAND SAW

EDGE OF WOOD BLOCK

CUT FROM BACK OF BOX
(TYP)

7³⁄₈"

7⁵⁄₈"

OPPOSING FORCES
PATTERN A

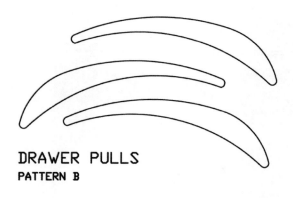

DRAWER PULLS
PATTERN B

SCALE IMAGE UP BY 175%

SPROUT BOX

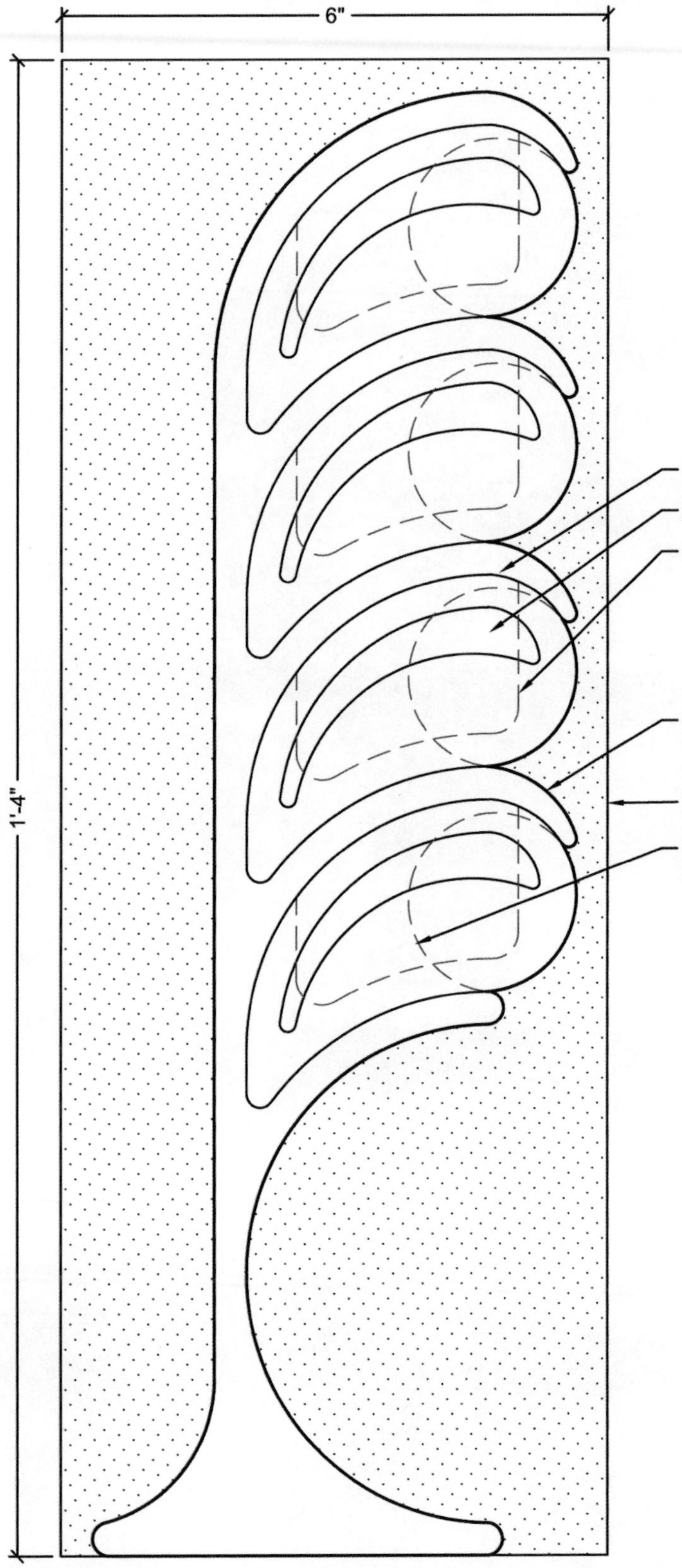

6"

1'-4"

DRAWER (TYP.)

DRAWER PULL (TYP.)

DRAWER CAVITY (TYP.)

PERIMETER OF BOX TO BE
CUT WITH THE BAND SAW

EDGE OF WOOD BLOCK

CUT FROM BACK OF BOX
(TYP)

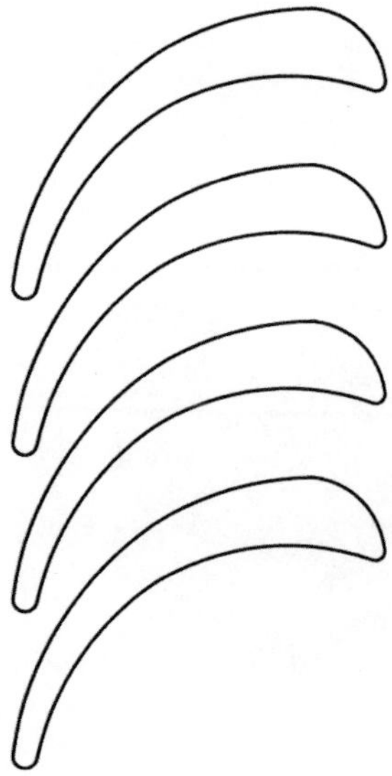

SPROUT
PATTERN A

DRAWER PULLS
PATTERN B

SCALE IMAGE UP BY 200%

GIVING TREE BOX

Key Steps

This box, and the few preceding boxes, have a unique element, the drawers are open on the ends. To give the box a little more shape, the back panel can be cut to reveal the drawers on the rear view.

Trace the cut out marks onto the back panel of the box. These are shown in the pattern, so try to match the shape, size, and location.

Use the band saw to cut the pieces free. Be careful not to cut the main arms of the box, just the back panel.

Opening the back up to reveal the drawers will mean that a portion of the back of the drawers need to be carved as well. To give ourselves a guide on how much carving is needed, insert the drawers into the box, then trace the shape of the box body onto the drawers with a pencil. At least that much of the back of the drawer needs to be carved.

Pencil guides can be very handy. In the image above, the carving limits for the drawer front have also been sketched onto the wood. The area inside the pencil marks will remain un-carved, which is an area just big enough for the drawer pulls to lay flat on the drawer front.

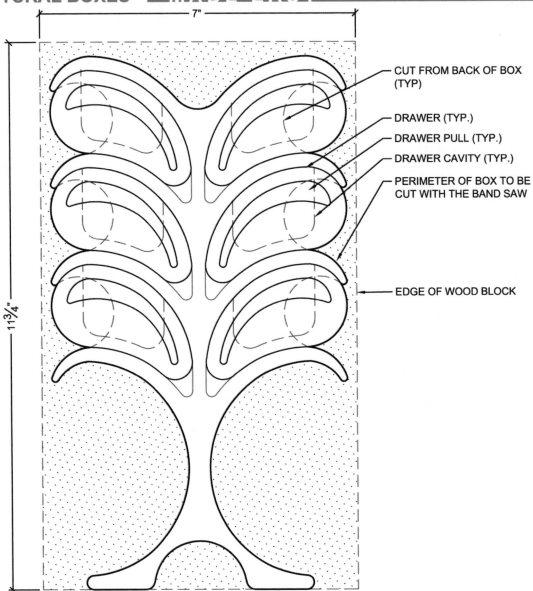

7"

11¾"

CUT FROM BACK OF BOX
(TYP)

DRAWER (TYP.)

DRAWER PULL (TYP.)

DRAWER CAVITY (TYP.)

PERIMETER OF BOX TO BE
CUT WITH THE BAND SAW

EDGE OF WOOD BLOCK

GIVING TREE
PATTERN A

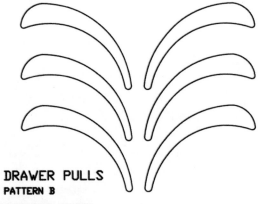

DRAWER PULLS
PATTERN B

SCALE IMAGE UP BY 200%

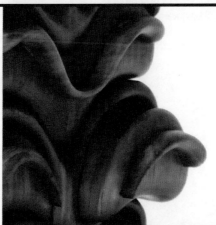

TRIBALISM BOX

Key Steps

This box and the one that follows it have one additional technique. Unlike the rest of the boxes where the body of the box is all one piece, these two boxes have two or more pieces to the main box body.

As with the rest of the boxes, the project starts with a stack of properly milled, glued, and taped boards. The outside edge of the box is cut with the band saw.

Removo the taped on back board with the putty knife. Then using the scroll saw, cut the box into segments as shown in the pattern. Also cut the drawer blanks.

When all the pieces of the box and the drawers have been cut free, glue the box body back together. Align the shaped edges of the box body with the back board of the box removed earlier. Clamp and let dry.

This box also has revealed drawer sides, so trace the shapes onto the inside of the back board with a marker as shown in the pattern, and cut these pieces free with the band saw.

Slice the drawer blanks to create the front and back sides of the drawers. Then cut the pocket from the middle section of the drawer blank. Then, glue and clamp the drawers together.

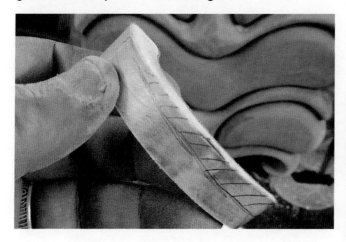

The 1" belt sander is used to remove the waste areas of the drawer pull. Then, the sander is used to rough shape the pulls.

Cut the drawer pulls from a piece of wood, For this box, we want the pulls to be thinner toward the inside of the box, tapering to full height on the outside edge. Pencil lines have been drawn on the pulls to indicate the amount of material to be sanded away.

Power sanders are used to refine and smooth the shapes.

Carve the rest of the box as usual. Attach the drawer pulls, and let dry. Finish in the desired manner. Another beautiful box is complete.

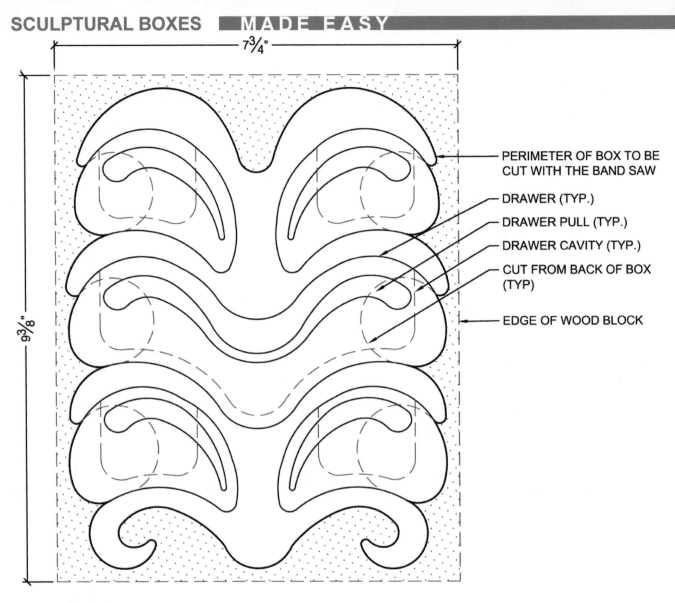

7 3/4"

9 3/8"

PERIMETER OF BOX TO BE
CUT WITH THE BAND SAW

DRAWER (TYP.)

DRAWER PULL (TYP.)

DRAWER CAVITY (TYP.)

CUT FROM BACK OF BOX
(TYP)

EDGE OF WOOD BLOCK

TRIBALISM
PATTERN A

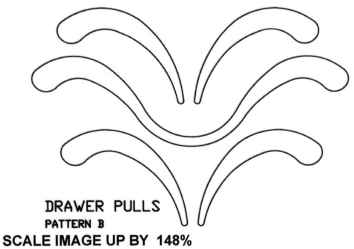

DRAWER PULLS
PATTERN B

SCALE IMAGE UP BY 148%

CONGRUENT WAVES BOX

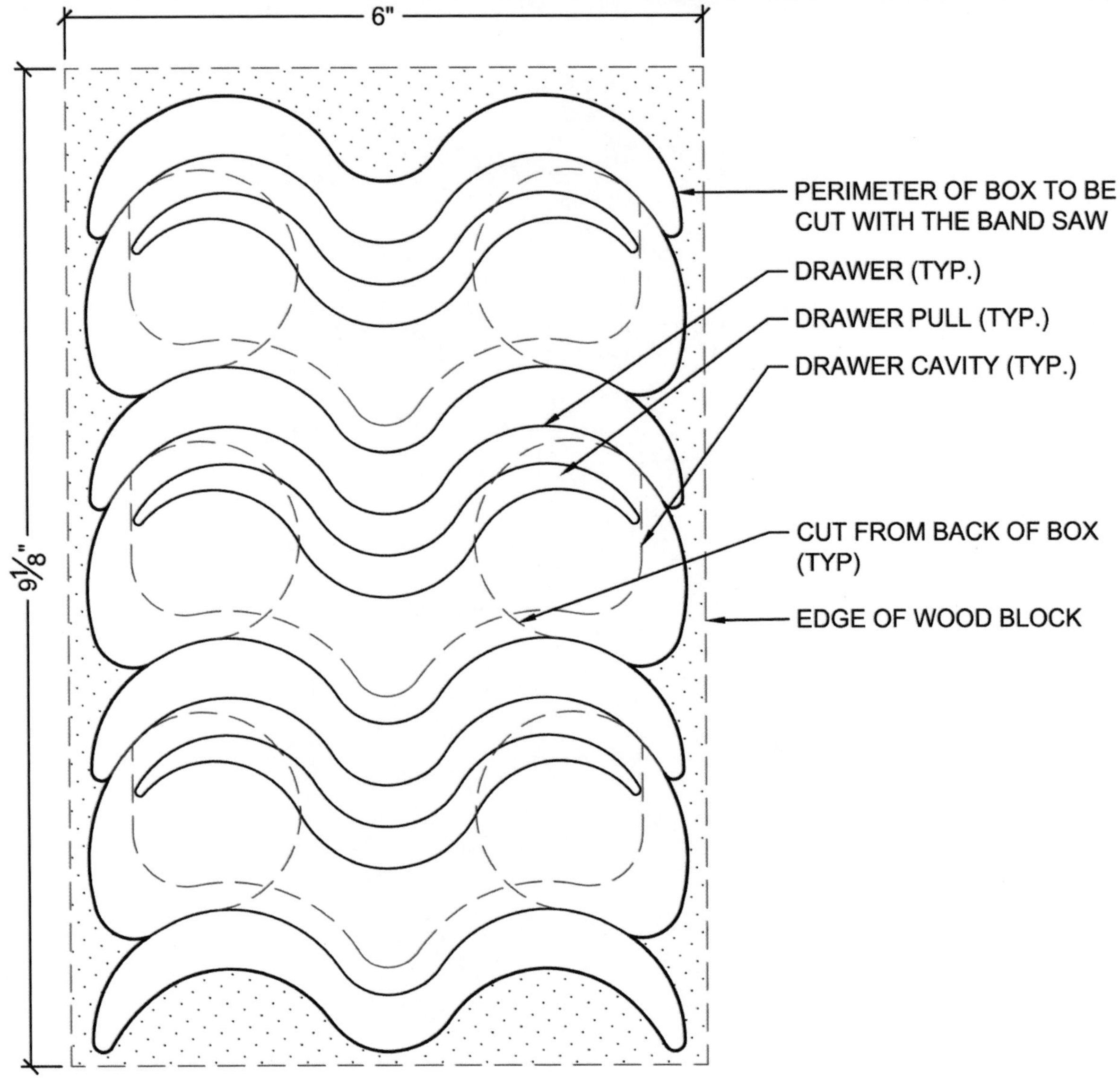

6"

9 1/8"

PERIMETER OF BOX TO BE
CUT WITH THE BAND SAW

DRAWER (TYP.)

DRAWER PULL (TYP.)

DRAWER CAVITY (TYP.)

CUT FROM BACK OF BOX
(TYP)

EDGE OF WOOD BLOCK

CONGRUENT WAVES
PATTERN A

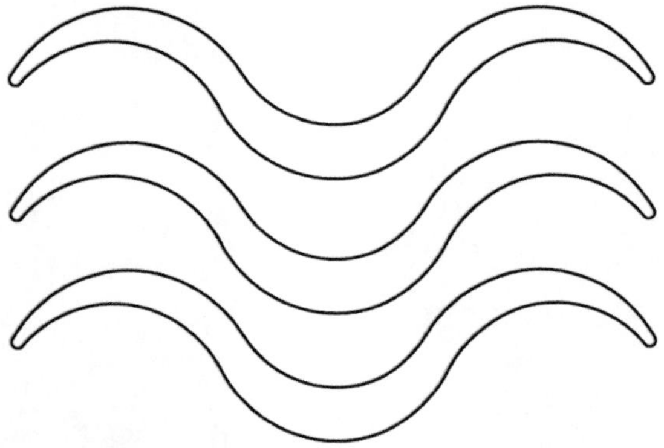

DRAWER PULLS
PATTERN B

SCALE IMAGE UP BY 130%

Printed in Great Britain
by Amazon